DON'T BE A PARENT, DON'T BE A FRIEND

7 THINGS TO REMEMBER AS PARENTS AND TEACHERS

LOKESH THAKUR

Dedication

To my parents, my brother, my teachers, and my school friends who made my childhood so amazing.

Contents

"No one is born fully formed: it is through self-experience in the world that we become what we are."

– Paulo Freire

Introduction

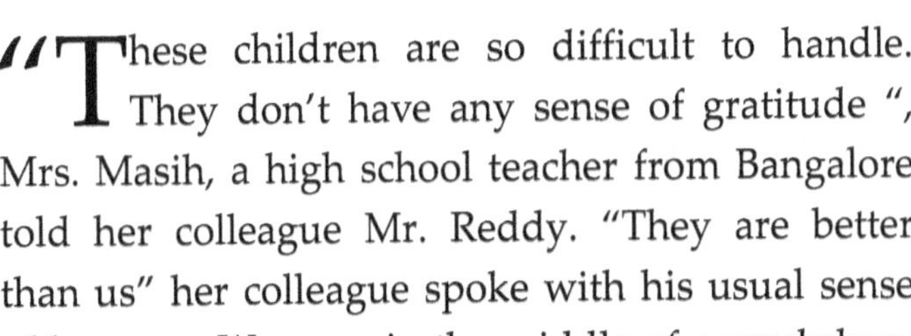

"These children are so difficult to handle. They don't have any sense of gratitude ", Mrs. Masih, a high school teacher from Bangalore told her colleague Mr. Reddy. "They are better than us" her colleague spoke with his usual sense of humour. We were in the middle of a workshop, planning for the next day's session. The conversation between these two teachers hung in my mind over the next few months.

For over two decades, my work as a School Principal, Teacher Educator, Journalist, and Writer has revolved around understanding children, teachers, and parents and supporting them in different aspects of education and life.

My work as a journalist covering education has allowed me to interact with thousands of students nationwide in different kinds of schools, from remote government schools to private schools in towns and cities, and some of the renowned institutions in metropolitan cities.

As a Teacher Educator, I have worked closely with teachers of all grades from kindergarten to college lectures.

Whenever I am asked to share my views on all such conversations that are mostly around childhood and how children nowadays are so difficult to handle, I mostly build my response with a statement that no two children are alike, and neither are the two different generations. Each generation has some interesting characteristics and ways of looking at life.

Interestingly both, children of the new generation and adults (children of previous generation) are constantly looking for guidance in handling each other. Is it possible to bridge the gap?

I mostly think around two points. One is to advise both groups to practice empathy. Do the two groups know each other well? Are they aware of each other's needs? Some things remain the same in all generations and some things are drastically different. So how do we look at these differences? In my experience youngsters are more open to listening and their views as compared to adults. They are more accepting of diversity. They are very clear on their needs and rights. They dare to take risks and try out new things. Parents and Teachers like it or not, must make some changes to the way they handle new generations. And most important they must appreciate new generations for all the great qualities they possess.

Second is the role teachers and parents play in the lives of children. There are areas where a new generation is struggling to handle things for which they are not fully responsible. We accept it or not, but parents and teachers are the creators of any society. How a child is going to live his or her life is primarily decided by his beliefs, thoughts, and daily practices that he or she develops in the first eighteen years of his or her life. That's the age where the influence of parents and teachers is maximum. Hence parents and teachers must understand how to handle the new generation. There are new age phrases like 'Teachers are friends now' 'Cool parents, cool kids', and 'Let's chill together' that show our changing approach as parents and teachers to handle new generation. Though there is nothing wrong with adapting ourselves to the needs of the new generation, it is equally important to remember that without a perspective, such tactics don't last long.

This book opens a new getaway to think about some of the key issues of parenting and teaching. Fears, comparisons, lack of conversations, and over-expectations are still at the core of parenting. These areas are critical not only during childhood but influence our lifelong journey.

Once you start reading the book, you will realize that some of the points will directly benefit you. In many cases, these may not work for you, or you may disagree without trying. It's fine. The purpose of this book is not to agree with my ideas or try the points shared by me as it is rather the goal is to help you think around the major issues of childhood.

One chapter 'Childhood in Crisis' is a reminder to all of us that we must start acting on the issue of addiction among our children. Hence this book is not just for teachers and parents but for each one of us who care for or about children. It is for anyone interested to understand how the epidemic of mental health is damaging our children's lives.

I hope this book will help each one of us to bond more deeply with our children and help them live their lives happily.

* * *

CHAPTER 1

Guardians Versus Ghosts

What is the most important need of any human being? Have you found yourself pondering on this question ever? If not, you must, it's a rather important one. When children are born, the priorities are to meet their basic needs and guarantee their safety Do we leave our newborn alone? Given all the hazards in our lives, why would we do that? Things always seem to find a way to make our lives harder. Not everyone has butterflies and rainbows. Anything bad can occur to us at any moment. Some events make us feel threatened, whether they are man-made or natural. We are constantly concerned about our security and safety. There are ups and downs in life. Anything nice today could be awful tomorrow. It is also fascinating to note that we live in a world where people compete with one another. Furthermore, this occurs not just in public settings but also in private ones, such as homes, schools, etc. There is always a perpetual danger of losing something. Our safety is a constant source of concern. The most vital thing in our life is a sense of safety and security.

Parents and Teachers provide that sense of security to us when we are not able to do things for ourselves. Parents and teachers give us a sense of belonging. They make us believe that they are ready to do anything to provide us with that sense of security and belongingness. We feel empowered when we are with them. They create a circle of safety for us, and they start growing us with this sense of security. They guard us from all kinds of dangers. Yes, Parents and Teachers are our real guardians in this world. We surrender ourselves to them believing that they will take care of us.

Parents and Teachers are the ones who offer us a feeling of community by accepting us for who we are. Not all but some of them even let us live our lives without restrictions. No matter where we go, our first need is always to feel protected and that's why we look for people whom we can trust. Allow me to share with you two fascinating true anecdotes that demonstrate the extent to which a teacher or parent go to save their children.

Mother's sacrifice for her daughter:
Savitri, a 45-year-old lady, spent her whole life in poverty. After her spouse passed away in 1999, she was compelled to take on odd jobs to support her family. In 2002, she started a small business selling

idly sambar in her village in the West Godavari district of Andhra Pradesh. She developed a profitable business and did tremendously well over the next three years. She was doing great and had a stable future financially, along with her two children, Kumari and Rangi. Kumari was seventeen and Ranga was fourteen. The two children also used to help their mother in their restaurant. The family's life was going smoothly until Kumari's health issues came out.

Both of her kidneys were failing, and the chances of her survival were less if the kidneys were not arranged. When her family first started looking for a donor, they were unable to find anyone.

Finding Kumari a kidney was essential because her condition was getting worse in the interim.

Hence Savitri decided to donate a kidney to her daughter. After getting a kidney from her mother, Kumari resumed her normal life within a few months. However, her mother, Savitri died in 2010 because of health complications brought on her by her single kidney.

Teacher's courage to save his student:
In 2018, the monsoon arrived in Kerala, the God's own country, a few days later than the usual monsoon season. It poured for several days on end. However, it started to storm heavily after two days,

causing havoc in Wayand, one of the most popular hill stations in Kerala. A massive landslide has claimed many lives. In the region of Idukki, 300 km away from the location of the landslide in the same state, a group of students were crossing a small river tributary. While crossing the river, students were holding hands, but the water was overflowing because of the heavy downpour. Mathew, a lecturer at the same college, was terrified of water, thus he avoided rivers at all costs. He asked a friend to bring a bike so they could go a long path without having to cross a river while he waited for the rain to stop. Suddenly, he heard students yelling as one of them was being washed when they were unexpectedly engulfed in a stream flow. Mathew, hydrophobic as he was, ran straight in to save his student. He started to struggle and seemed like he was about to drown, but he was gripping his student's hand tightly. For the next five minutes, both were limited to holding onto a tree. After some time, a few people from the neighbourhood went to the site holding a rope, and luckily both were rescued safely.

Both stories are great examples of a parent and a teacher putting themselves at risk for the sake of their kids. There can be examples where other people might have done this for others but the level a parent and a teacher can go to help his or her kid is incomparable.

The point I want to make is that teachers and parents are there to guard their kids and that is their biggest role in our lives.

They are guardians of our life.

The problem starts happening when parents and teachers start using their ways to protect their children. One of the most common ways is to protect our children through fear.

The adults (mostly parents and teachers) in our lives teach fear to us. All children pick up the habit of avoiding new situations if their parents' express anxiety or display other indicators of fear towards them. Most of the children pick up a phobia by observing their parents' reactions to them. For example, a youngster may become too fearful to travel alone because of repeated reminders to 'be careful' in the outside world. The degree to which children feel free to be who they are and confidently explore the world is also influenced by the actions of adults. Harsh parenting, which includes both physical and verbal abuse, is linked to worse results for kids, such as underachievement in school, increased anxiety and aggression, and strained peer relationships.

Similarly, teachers also play a crucial role in the development of fear responses among kids.

Many students feel nervous or afraid in different ways when they are in the classroom. We often label the new generation as bold, carefree, and rude, what we forget is that there are different sides to their personalities. If we don't pass judgments just based on our observations and spend time knowing them, we will understand how even the boldest student in the class has some kind of fear. Different students feel nervous or afraid in different ways when they are in school Many adjust quickly but many are always in fear. Fear starts interfering with their capacity to learn in school. In many cases, some children have persistent or chronic anxiety and fear, which can make it difficult for them to comprehend their books, needed for academic success.

Many children believe that they could perform poorly, and they are excessively afraid of it. Even the toppers or high performers are clouded by the anxiety of washing out on the next unit test or exam.

Some students are always worried. They tell themselves, "My classmates are going to do better than me" and become unduly stressed out by the need to outperform others to receive passing grades. Children often exhibit excessive shyness or even fear of being singled out during class. Many of us experience a syndrome called gelotophobia, which is the fear of being laughed at by others. The seeds of this syndrome are sowed in our childhood.

Many students even have anxieties that are reinforced by their caste, culture, and region.

Any student under any kind of fear responds negatively. These reactions or responses are often seen in three ways:

1. **Cognitively:** Many children are unable to focus or concentrate, think unnecessarily, and replay difficult events from the past in their minds.

2. **Emotionally:** Easily agitated, overcome by excessive nervousness, frustration, and other negative feelings.

3. **Physiologically:** Shortness of breathing, shaking of legs, stomach-ache, headache

Fear also leads to disruptive practices in the classroom, incomplete assignments, repeated absences or not responding to adults' questions.

Most kids these days are in some form of anxiety. We often keep hearing that children are depressed. The cases of suicides have increased. There have been instances where teenagers are involved in heinous crimes. And if you try to connect anxiety, depression, suicide, and crime, out of many factors, one common factor is an imagination of anxious feelings. The moment we start anticipating that something wrong is going to happen we start worrying and do unrepairable things.

Let's try to understand how kids are in constant worry and state of anxiety.

Rohit was the son of a doctor couple in a small town of Punjab. He was brilliant in his studies and a topper throughout his school days. On his first attempt, he got into a good medical college. Parents were happy that their wish of making their child a doctor had come true. After getting into college Rohit got freedom as he was staying away from his parents. When he was at home he was never allowed to go out of home after 8 pm. His parents were very strict and always threatened him to go outside. There were many other restrictions on him also. He was not allowed to go to the cinema or eat dinner outside. Once he became independent in college he started hanging out with friends at night. Though he was in a constant state of worry about his parents' disapproval of late-night parties, he was enjoying his new life. One fine evening he went to a bar with his friends. Out of five friends, Rohit and another friend had never drunk in their lives. They had ordered their favorite Korean dishes. All were happily enjoying the party. Suddenly a fight erupted in the bar between staff of the bar and some customers. The arguments got heated and there was a fistfight. After some time, the police came. Meanwhile, some people have started recording the incident on camera. Rohit noticed this. Since they were having food, Rohit did not leave the place at that time. After the incident, Rohit was in constant worry that if his parents got to know about this, what would he say? Why had he gone to Bar? Did he also drink? Why did he not leave the bar when the fight happened? What was the reason for going out for dinner? For some days he was just depressed and kept thinking about whether his parents would get to know about this incident or not. One day while speaking to his parents, his father mentioned that he must take care of his friend circle and should not hang out much with his friends. He also warned him about alcohol and pub culture. That night Rohit committed suicide. A small note was found in his notebook that mentioned that he could no longer take the guilt of breaking his parents' trust.

Naina and Reena were students in grade 8 in a government high school in the remote village of Pilibhit, district of Uttar Pradesh. Both were average students in their studies. Naina's parents were always concerned about her marks and her teachers also often complained about her behaviour in the classroom. On many occasions, Naina's father would scold her in the evening for not studying properly. On Baisakhi festival, the whole village was busy celebrating the festival. Naina had received the unit test marks and she had not performed well in the exams. Parents' meeting was due after the Baisakhi festival. That evening she called her friend Reena who was also worried due to her poor marks. Both friends planned to flee from their homes. Two girls took an auto to the bus station, then took a bus to Bareilly, and then boarded a train to Amritsar where Naina's uncle used to live. They were noticed on the train by TT who informed the police and then handed the two girls to their parents.

In July 2024, 15 years in Gurgaon stabbed his childhood friend to death because of jealousy. He was chatting with a girl for a few months. After some days he got to know that his childhood friend was also talking to the same girl. As he felt jealous, he planned to murder his childhood friend. He bought a knife for Rs. 150, called his friend on the pretext of a party, and then committed murder by stabbing him with the knife.

If you analyse these three incidents you will find that one of the common things in these three cases was fear.

Fear of shame, fear of losing self-worth, and fear of abandonment. Let's explore a bit on fear.

Fear is a natural reaction of our body when the body gets signals of any threat. It is a very common emotion and plays an important role in our safety. The problem is when fears manufactured by our imaginations start dictating our lives. There can be numerous forms of fear but generally, there are five major forms of fear.

1. **Fear of death:** The moment we feel that our life is at risk we get the fear of death.

2. **Fear of getting physical pain:** The fear of losing any part of our body is another form of form that we experience in our lives.

3. **Fear of losing our autonomy:** The moment we feel that we are stuck inside a room or a building lift or any place from where the chances of going out are minimal, we start fearing losing our autonomy. The same happens when we are stuck in a job or a relationship.

4. **Fear of abandonment:** This is the worst kind of fear that is most common among youngsters. The moment we feel abandoned and rejected we start fearing that no one would need us. Nobody would value us, and we are left alone to die in our lives.

5. **Fear of losing our self-respect:** Whenever we feel embarrassed, humiliated, ashamed, and guilty we are in fear of losing our self-respect. We feel that we will no longer be valued.

Many other emotions have a strong connection with fear. For example, Anger is a secondary emotion that starts with fear. Similarly, jealousy occurs when we fear either abandonment or losing our self-respect. Jealousy is a common reason for crimes in youngsters and even in adults. Most of the crimes linked to relationships happen due to jealousy and jealousy has strong connections with fear.

Even look at the larger picture. Religious, racial, and caste-based hatred has a linkage with fear. Fear of losing identities. I am not saying that it is the only reason, but it does have a connection with fear which is often imaginary.

The main problem is with the memories of fear. Our brain stores our memories of fear very strongly and that's the reason why we avoid doing many things only because of memories of fear. Kids are not ready to go to school or the hospital or outside home or skip exams. In most of the cases, they have a fear of being in an uncomfortable situation.

How should we handle fear?

As I said earlier, fear is a basic emotion and important for our survival but if used as a controlling tool, it damages childhood.

Don't Be A Parent, Don't Be A Friend: Be A Mentor

1. Help children to identify their fears:
We must help our kids to experience fear as a basic human reaction and should consciously handle it. Kids should be made aware of different kinds of fear and the role it plays in our lives which is to warn and protect us. This can be done by allowing our kids to identify their fears. Instead of getting frightened and controlling, we must use it as a tool for better preparation for any possible risk or threat. Kids must be guided on how day-to-day insecurity of small things in their lives could lead to chronic stress and anxiety.

2. Educate them about fear and its impact:
It is important to have sessions around learning and fear for our kids. Does fear come from inside naturally or do we acquire it from surroundings, or are we taught to be afraid? Some fears are natural, some are learned from our surroundings, and some are fed inside us. For example, fear of pain in the body is natural but fear of getting lost in the crowd comes through our experiences of any incident and we learn from our past incidents. In some cases, fear is fed inside us. For example, ghost stories. We have never seen ghosts still we all fear ghosts. Even our

parents have never seen ghosts, but they also fear ghosts. We are taught to fear things that even exist or not we are not sure of. That's how fear is taught or created in our minds. Similarly, the fear of other communities even if we have no experience we are taught by our parents, teachers, and other people in our surroundings to fear them.

3. Be proactive in sharing about your worries and feelings:

We frequently neglect to spend quality time with our children because of our hectic schedules. Children are also more comfortable communicating their issues with their friends rather than with parents and teachers. If we, parents and teachers take the initiative to talk to our kids about our difficulties, worries, and anxieties, they will begin to confide in us as well. Assuring kids that we will not criticize or hold them accountable instead of understanding them will go a long way toward reducing their anxiety.

The most crucial thing for parents and teachers to keep in mind is that fear dictates the decisions we make in life. Either we give up, get despondent, lose hope, or take action to make things better. Therefore, we must help our children in understanding this. Ultimately, we are our children's guardians, giving them safety rather than ghosts that frighten them.

* * *

The Consequences Of Comparisons

Supriya of Kanpur, Uttar Pradesh got married to Vivek Malhotra in December 2017. It was an arranged marriage. Supriya had worked for a bank for two years before quitting her job to become a full-time housemaker. Vivek was a Chartered Accountant in Lucknow. Vivek's father had died when he was in school. His mother struggled hard for her son's education. She worked as a teacher in a school to support her son's education. It was obvious that to Vivek, his mother was like a god. He always used to show gratitude towards his mother. On the other hand, Supriya was brought up in a joint family. Along with his parents and two siblings, his two uncles' families also used to stay in the same house. Supriya was a very shy and sensitive child. Her parents often used to compare her with the rest of the kids in the family who were extroverts. Because of this, her self-esteem was very low. She would hardly speak when she was a child. Later in college she grew as a rebel and had fights with her parents and other siblings regularly. She often used to feel lonely. After marriage, things were going fine for the first few months as Vivek was a true gentleman. Like his mother, Vivek was a very hard-working and caring person. He would help Supriya in household work. He would care for her well-being, was soft-spoken, and a family person. He was in a well-to-do job as well.

Slowly tension started happening between Supriya and Vivek as Vivek would often bring her mother's example for any work. If Supriya would cook something delicious, Vivek would say that her mother's cooking is the best in the world. If Supriya planned for a movie Vivek would talk and give an example of his childhood when his mother used to take him to picnics. Supriya's parents had thought that marriage would give stability to Supriya, and she would get a sense of security after getting a partner. Sadly, things worsened after marriage.

In March 2018, Vivek's mother had gone to Varanasi for a family function. Vivek had a lot of office work due to the March closing work in the Bank and hence he was not able to help Supriya in the kitchen. He was having breakfast in the morning, and he was getting late to the office, but he was a patient person so instead of panicking he called his supervisor and told him that he would be late to the office. At 10 am he left for office. Before leaving the office, he told Supriya not to worry about making food saying that his mother would come tomorrow so she would handle things well. He wanted to ensure Supriya that she does not have to struggle much in household work. At 11 am he called Supriya to enquire about electricity bill payment. Her phone kept on ringing multiple times but there was no response. From 11 to 11: 45 am he called her number more than 30 times but no response yet. Finally, he rushed home and found the door locked. With the help of neighbors when he broke the house, he found his wife hanging from the ceiling of the roof. There was a small note on the table.

I wish my parents, and my husband had accepted me. Before marriage, my parents used to compare me to my siblings. After marriage, my husband compares me to his mother.

I wish I was good enough so that nobody compares me to anyone.

Vivek was in disbelief at how someone could commit suicide for such a minor thing.

Like Supriya, many people suffer their whole life asking for their acceptance by their surroundings. One of the biggest reasons for this is the comparisons done by their families, teachers, and other people when they were children.

Why do parents and teachers compare?

As we discussed in the first chapter parents and teachers are the ones who would go to any level to help their children do well in their life. Sadly, doing well in life is linked to doing well in studies when we are kids. To motivate kids' parents and teachers often give examples of other students who have done well. ' Uski tarah bano', ' Verma ji ka ladka kitna mehnati hai'., Sharma ji ki bitiya ke toh 98% marks aaye hain '. Even within families' comparisons are done between siblings. Bade bhai se kuch sikho. Bada Layak Chhota Nalayak. Hamara Chhota beta to hoshiar hai but bada thoda kamjoor hai. Even the same is done in schools by teachers. 'Look at Rahul, he has done brilliant work. Can everyone be like him?

It is not just grades and studies the comparison is done in other areas of life also. For example, many parents pass comments to their kids on their appearance and behavior. 'Bhikhari ki tarah dikh raha hai'. Teachers often say- Majnu bna firta hai. Girls are often taunted as khud ko 'Katrina Kaif samjhti hai' These comments in the form of comparison are often taken lightly by everyone without realizing that they create deep scars inside us.

There is no question mark on the intention behind this. Parents and teachers dream of seeing their children do well in their studies and they think by giving examples of others there will be changes in them also. Unfortunately, it works the other way around.

Here are some of the serious consequences of comparisons.

- **The feeling of jealousy and rivalry:**

  Most of the kids who are compared with their siblings and friends develop a feeling of jealousy and rivalry towards others. They grow up as extremely insecure people and instead of working on their capabilities, they are often thinking about other's success.

- **Ignored Child:**

  Childhood is a very sensitive period. Whenever children are compared to others, they feel ignored and not valued. This leads to a strong sense of detachment among kids towards their families. As they grow up, they look for love and belongings in the outside world. Many teenagers and adults often get trapped in wrong relationships as they are always looking for people who can accept them as they are.

- **Low self-esteem and self-worth:**

  'I am not good enough' is one of the most common lines that I have heard from most teenagers who are very creative people. When

I tell them that their work is good, they feel happy but do not accept my words. They have such low self-esteem and self-worth that they don't try new things. Because of this reason, many talented kids fail to do well in their lives as they are always in self-doubt. They are always judging themselves because their parents and teachers have done this with them many times. Yes, knowingly or unknowingly parents pass judgment on kids' behaviour, actions, personalities, and character. Whenever any comparison is done by any parent and teacher it is taken as a judgement by children. Ask any child how he or she feels when compared to others. He or she will say I don't like it. I hate it. We fail to understand in what situation comparison is fruitful and when it is dangerous. Comparisons are useful when we must select things out of many. For example, when we must buy a new product, we compare existing products and then reach a conclusion. Similarly, when we must select a candidate for a vacancy we do comparisons. But comparisons when done to foster someone's learning are devastating as they make children feel inferior and bad and sometimes, they fail to come out of that inferiority complex their whole life.

- **The Anxious Generation:**

The world has become a rat race, and comparisons have put the emotional health of children and youngsters at very high risk. Most new generation people are highly anxious and out of many reasons one key reason is their fear of losing to other people. 'Somebody will take the limelight', 'What will happen to me', 'Everyone is shining on Instagram but I don't have followers'. Millions of people who scroll through social media every day end up feeling unaccomplished. We have started defining ourselves through the lens of others.

The whole business of 'likes and followers' is dangerously pushing the new generation into serious anxiety issues but remember the seeds of this anxiety are sowed by our parents and teachers when they first start comparing the kids to others.

- **Strained Relationships:**

As we noticed above in the case study of Supriya how her childhood comparisons kept on triggering her mental health and even after finding a good partner, she felt inadequate ultimately taking a step to end her own life. The danger of comparison is not just up to one individual rather it spoils all relationships. The emotional baggage is too huge to be unloaded and destroys the lives of many people.

Don't Be A Parent, Don't Be A Friend: Be A Spiritual Guru

Many of my known people have joined spiritual groups where they go every week. They are highly committed to their communities. I don't go anywhere and would not recommend anyone to join such communities but there are some learnings from these communities which we can apply with our children also. Here are the top three practices to think about:

Start practicing self-love:

One major difference people find after joining these communities is about how they feel about themselves. Most of these spiritual organizations tell them that human beings are special people, and they are part of a superpower. God is within each human and most important within each human being. This feeling that I am a special person and part of a larger superpower is extremely useful for any human being. It is a step towards self-love. It teaches us to value ourselves first. We must love ourselves because we are part of the universe. Now remove the second part which can be debatable and focus on the first part. We must love ourselves.

We have often seen youngsters posing themselves in front of the camera. They just love it. It is so important for any human to shower some amount of self-love. Remember each child is unique. No two humans are alike. Teach your kids to practice self-love the way spiritual communities tell their members to do. Tell them they are not here to compare themselves with others but rather to live their own life their way. It is their life, and they must love it.

Processes are more important than results

Another important lesson that we can learn from these communities is that they stick to their processes. They don't waste time arguing with each other. Will it happen or not happen? They are extremely dedicated to what we call 'service'. Each member of the community follows the processes strictly and that is the most beautiful part of these communities. This is an excellent example of a growth mindset. It is this part that people like the most. They are fully engaged in this and that makes them feel happy and growing.

We must help the kids to develop this kind of growth mindset where the focus should be processes rather than results. The moment we think about results first we will get into the trap of a rat race. After any hard work don't focus just on the results but rather on the whole process. Ask them whether they are enjoying the processes or not. Can you share three things that you are learning while following these processes? Help kids understand that the more they focus on processes happier and more successful they will be.

Self-reflection is the key.

Another remarkable feature of these spiritual communities is their guru's ability to make his followers think about themselves. All members are asked to think: What are we doing in this world? What is our goal? What do we want to achieve? The moment a guru asks this question the followers start the process of self-reflection. Self-reflection has amazing power. Just try the same with your kids. Every child has a goal or dream. Ask your kid to think about those dreams or goals. Tell them to think about their present situation what they are right now and future goals and what they want to become. After putting in some effort ask them to reflect on their practice so that they can track their progress. Am I better than yesterday? Whenever they see progress ask them to acknowledge it, feel good about it, and continue to work towards their goal. Remember self-reflection leads to satisfaction whereas comparison leads to sadness.

* * *

CHAPTER 3

The Power Of Conversations

A few years ago, I went to a Bengali-inhabited area in my locality in Uttarakhand to witness the Durga Puja festival. I had seen the Durga Puja in Kolkata and was overwhelmed by the cultural richness of the festival. There was no other festival that mesmerized me so much. It was a festival beyond religious identities where people from all religious backgrounds had come to attend the grand affair. When I got to know that a huge number of Bengali-speaking people live in this area, I went with a lot of enthusiasm to see the same. As I entered the first village where Pandal was made I found only a couple of craftsmen doing some work. To my surprise, there were very less people. I thought that I had arrived in time as there were very less children. As I decided to walk towards the next village, I saw dozens of children sitting near the Durga Temple. There was no light, maybe the electricity had gone. I was surprised to see so many young boys sitting in darkness. All of them were glued to their smartphones. Some of them were my students but none of them noticed me. Suddenly one of the students noticed me and shocked by my visit came closer to me and enquired about my visit. When I asked them how long they all have been on smartphones. They said that it's been four to five hours. I was just astounded to hear this. It was not an ordinary day but one of the biggest festivals of their community and they all are busy spending time on screens.

Though I was shocked that day, we all know that online addiction is a real thing now. Most children nowadays almost constantly use smartphones. Even when they are doing something else, they are thinking about social media which means that the average 15-16 hours they spend per day on social media.

It is because of this level of constant use of social media that they are so addicted to our smartphones that they stop whatever we are doing and immediately rush to check our phones.

Out of many things that kids have stopped doing nowadays, the thing that comes to me first is conversation with the people around them.

It has become a common thing for any of us to interrupt a face-to-face conversation even when there is a small message on our phone. We have become so obsessed with smartphones that we have lost the art of talking. And it is not just true for kids. Even parents do the same. Most of the parents when talking to their kids are flipping through their phones. What is the message they are giving to the kids? You are less important than the update or video on my phone. Due to this behaviour, there is very little importance given to talking or conversations. That's why most young people feel isolated. The relationships between friends have become superficial. It's all a virtual world out there and no one cares what's happening in the real world in their surroundings. Sometimes it seems that everyone is a zombie, completely absorbed in their smartphones.

Interestingly when I talk to Parents and Teachers about this issue most of them say that they do talk to their kids regularly. Very rarely does anyone accept that the conversation has reduced.

Here comes another important issue. Not only is the quantity of talks reduced but there is a drastic decrease in the quality of talks.

How do parents and teachers talk to kids nowadays?

It is mostly to pass a message. We are always in a hurry to get things done. The whole point of conversation is just to say what we want to say without even realizing whether another person is listening to us or not. We are so much into our work that we don't realize how the conversation is going on. The conversations nowadays are just for getting the responses or getting our work done. We often forget here that children catch things from us. They learn more from our behaviour and words than through textbooks. Let me share an interesting example from one of the incidents I witnessed a few years ago.

I went to one of my students Nita's home to talk to her parents. When I entered her home, I saw her going out of the home. I sat near the veranda waiting for her return. Meanwhile, I saw her two younger siblings- a 6-year-old Dev and a 2-year-old Raju. Dev was coloring a picture in his notebook while Raju was making a mess out of colors. Dev was getting irritated and lost his temper and pushed Raju away. Raju started crying. Suddenly I saw their mother coming from inside pulling the ear of Dev and abusing him with a local gaali'. Dev stood still for a moment and then threw away all his colors towards Raju with the same abusive word. I had come to talk about Nita's similar behaviour in the class. For the last few weeks, she has been using the same word in the classroom.

That's why the quality of conversations is so important. If we don't talk properly with our kids, they will just pick what they listen to and use the words as it is.

The power of conversations:
The quality conversations have a profound impact on children's lives. Conversations are the building blocks of relationships between children and adults. One of the main objectives of conversation between adults and children is to make children feel heard and understood. This is crucial for children to speak freely. If they speak freely their language will surely improve. Moreover, their connection with you will become better. The best teachers in the world are the ones who listen to their kids and kids talk to them freely. Similarly, happy kids often have parents who allow their kids to express their feelings freely.

At present the whole exercise of schooling is to focus on everyone's achievement. Social skills and collaborative learning are at the backstage. Even parents want their children to learn new skills to excel in competitions. Time is money is the new mantra and parents want their kids to just be more productive. There is so much academic stress among children. For civil service preparations, parents have started sending kids to coaching right after high school. There is no time and mental space for socialization and making honest, deep relationships.

In fact, in the last few years after COVID-19 one of the drastic changes I have noticed in kids is their lack of empathy towards others which is quite opposite to what was expected. Covid taught us that the world is uncertain, and we need each other in difficult times but surprisingly I found a few basic things missing from most of the youngsters. Firstly, most of the youngsters are unable to recognize their actual emotions and understand them. Most of them just say that they feel lost. They are not bothered about any other person except their own mental space. They are struggling to understand that their mental space will not help them to come out of their emotional issues. Empathy towards others has vanished and it has also resulted in kids becoming isolated from others. I found the lack of quality conversation among adults and children as main reason for this problem.

Do we talk to children about their feelings and emotions? Do we help them express their feelings properly? Do we teach them to be compassionate towards themselves and others? Do we ask them whether they empathize with others in the same emotional struggles or not?

If our answer to any of the questions is No, then we as adults should not talk about our society lacking empathy.

Another important objective conversation plays in our lives is to make our society better. Yes, the type of conversations we have with children influences them a lot in their lives. It is through conversations that children learn new things in life. They understand the people around them and care for them. They become confident and independent. They learn to maintain relationships. They accept different kinds of people in their surroundings. They become more tolerant of others. Instead of competing with others, they collaborate with others.

Just look at a few of the most common sentences we often hear.

- It is a selfish world, so be selfish.
- No one is here to help us.
- The world is bad and hence don't make friends.

- If you must survive, you must be better than others.
- We must give a damn to the world to succeed.
- Our communities/caste/religion are pure, others are not.

Do we feel that we can make a better world if we keep conversing along these lines with our kids?

Now just think the opposite if we use these sentences with kids.

- It's a beautiful world.
- Everyone is unique.
- Whenever someone is in pain, we should help him or her.
- We must respect everyone equally.
- Even if someone harms us, we must forgive them.

The world around us is made by the kind of conversation we have with people around us. Childhood is the stage when things are picked up quickly. If we don't work around conversations with children just imagine how the world will become. Social media is teaching children to become self-obsessed.

Everyone wants to be an influencer qualified by likes and followers without any sense of social purpose. Do we want our kids to become selfish individuals who have no sense of community? Do we want kids to grow up without having collective experiences? Do we want our kids to disconnect with each other in such a way that we share our moments of joy and sorrow through virtual meetings? Do we want our kids to judge their lives based on their likes and followers in the virtual world?

If the answer to any of these questions is No then we must use the power of conversations, or else it will be too late.

Don't Be a Parent, Don't Be a Friend: Be a Facilitator

- Instead of talking to get things done or being busy on smartphones, can we start talking to our kids with the same curiosity they show when they are growing up? No smartphones while talking. Set the rule before talking.

- Ask kids what they like and what they don't like and share your likes and dislikes also.

- Allow them to agree and disagree. Help them understand that disagreement is not rejecting someone's idea but rather placing another point of view.

- Encourage them to look for solutions to the problems instead of giving them answers straight away.

- Help them to empathize with other people's lives and ask about their feelings when they do something miserable.

- Share your concerns when you want to caution them for any misdeed in the form of probabilities and possibilities.

- Discuss books and movies. Talk about characters, plots, etc.

* * *

CHAPTER 4

Learning From The Mistakes

Devika was one of the shyest girls in grade 6. She was silent most of the time. She would never indulge in any disruptive behaviour in class. She was punctual and would arrive on time, sit calmly in the class, and would not go outside the class unless it was urgent. She was a sweet little child who would support teachers without creating any problems in the classroom. But there was an issue with her. She would never answer whenever teachers ask questions. She would also never do homework. Despite teachers trying hard to understand the reasons, she did not change. Despite her parents telling her to stop her school she did not respond. When I was joined as the principal of this extremely democratic school, I asked for the list of students who don't cooperate with teachers. Her name was in that list of 50-plus students at the bottom. When I enquired about her case, unlike other kids who were disruptive, she was found to be extremely calm and easy except that she would not respond to the questions asked in the classroom while teaching. She will never do the homework. Because of this, her overall learning level was very poor. Meanwhile, I met her a couple of times on the way to school as she used to come a bit early to school. I gave her a lift which she reluctantly accepted. She was soft-spoken and responded well to my simple questions about her life in general. Since I found her easy going and her class teacher had less interest in working with her, I took the responsibility of helping her out. In the next few months what I found was a perfect example of how parents and teachers themselves become barriers to their kids' learning and that too mostly unknowingly, unintentionally. When Devika was in early grades, in classes 2 and 3 in another school, her class teacher used to point out mistakes in her homework with a red pen. Her notebook would be full of red lines. It was a routine behaviour from her teacher at school. At home, her grandfather would ask her questions and whenever she would answer wrong, she would be scolded. Sometimes he would beat her up also. For some years this continued, and the little child continued to struggle like this. Later when she joined our school where it was not allowed for teachers to use red pen or put lines in children's notebooks. However, her fear of getting scolded and labelled as a person with maximum mistakes has put a deep scar on her personality. That's the reason why she would never answer any question either in writing or in oral. Many such students in our classrooms are victims of this behaviour from adults.

Pointing out mistakes or Finding fault in children's work is often the favourite work of adults because they think that they are helping kids to learn and improve without knowing that they are damaging them.

Why mistakes are important in learning?

Can anyone learn without committing mistakes? Even God must have also made some mistakes while creating this beautiful world. Jokingly but let's accept that whenever anyone is creating anything or learning anything, mistakes are bound to happen. Some make mistakes once or twice, but many learn from repeated mistakes. We have already discussed in the previous chapter that no two individuals are alike. So how their learning pattern will be similar? We must see mistakes as learning moments that our children need to go through in their lives to grow into happy and successful adults. Our children should learn to make the correct decisions in the future without the fear of punishment. If we help them discover the difference between good and wrong and give them the proper freedom to explore those ideas without getting fearful of mistakes, it will teach them valuable lessons that will last a lifetime.

Pointing mistakes lead to self-doubts:
Nobody likes to make mistakes in front of others. Even we adults dislike it, hate it because we all want to avoid falling to maintain our sense of self and identity. When parents and teachers point out our mistakes, especially in the presence of others it impacts children's confidence and sends them down trauma spirals of internalized inadequacies. They start developing a preconceived notion about their ability to learn and very often it limits their views and prospects for a lifetime. Most of the people who fail to do things they like in their lives are because of one single thought of not committing mistakes. Because of this self-doubt which is fed inside them by their teachers and parents, they will never take risks. For them committing mistakes is another step to self-doubt. They have accepted that they are not good and hence whatever they do will never be good. This image that I commit mistakes when I do things. This belief that I will never succeed because I am

not good. This thought that what will happen if I fail to do things well. The fear of failure that comes from self-doubt is one of the most common reasons why many talented and hard-working people don't try new things. Just think if these creative and hardworking people try doing things that they love to do how beautiful their lives will be and that will also give happiness to the people around them.

Mistakes are frustrating but pointing out mistakes is devastating:

As Parents and Teachers, we want our children to learn well and do things right. When we try to teach them anything new and when they don't perform as per our expectations, we get frustrated. The more mistakes they commit, the more frustrated they become. And it is not only us that are getting frustrated, but even children also themselves get frustrated a lot.

Even when we assure them that there is no right or wrong when starting, or that with practice they'll get better and better, many children still suffer distress.

They must go through this phase of committing mistakes, getting frustrated, and learning from them. Otherwise, how would they deal with the overwhelming distress from the failure in the real world?

Now the most important thing here is that we should allow them to experience this on their own. If we start pointing out mistakes in them again and again, they will not be ready to accept society and the world. If they are told that there is no place for mistakes in this world, they will start hating the world itself. That's how many youngsters and adults become anti-social. They accept that this world is not for them. Many of them get confused, succumb to drug addiction and some even commit suicide. Many of them grow into individuals who hate the world around them because their mistakes are labelled as crimes by their parents and teachers, and they start believing that they are criminals and that's how they need to live in this world.

Don't Be A Parent, Don't Be A Friend: Be A Trainer

- Parents and Teachers must practice activities that include children in problem-solving skills. The non-linear nature of problem-solving is that it helps parents and teachers cultivate tolerance towards mistakes in their students as learners have to start, stop, pause, perplex, draft, modify, and rethink while solving any problem. As their tolerance grows, children become more adept learners who not only freely accept mistakes as a necessary component of learning but also recognize their inherent value.

- Often, the greatest method for our children to pick up lessons from their own is through committing mistakes. Allow that process to unfold when your children face a natural consequence for their mistakes and then take responsibility for them.

- Help your children create a plan of restitution if their mistakes have caused harm to them or someone else.

- Teach them the value of offering an apology without making them feel guilty or fearful about their mistakes.

- Sometimes some children react differently to mistakes and instead of learning from the mistakes they become physically aggressive, start lying, distance themselves from their close ones, and even try to harm themselves. Here comes the importance of conversation that we have already discussed in the previous chapter 'The Power of Conversations.

- Help them to recognize and accept their emotions so that they can make positive changes in their behaviour. This is crucial because if children learn to handle these feelings at a young age, they will be able to deal with their whole life.

* * *

Life Is Not Fair But Beautiful

We all know that life is not fair, and the world is so imbalanced. Inequalities due to caste, colour, race, sex, poverty, region, health and political influence, and many other areas of life are all too common. Why then do we feel such a strong feeling of duty to treat our children fairly on all occasions? Parents and teachers just want what is best for them. Though it is hard to keep kids in a bubble, what lessons would they learn even if we could? Is it not a wiser step to share about the hard realities of life with our kids? Our children need our support in realizing that equity and fairness are not always present in life.

Life is not fair because everyone is competitive against each other.

Despite our desire to deny it, we are all in a competitive environment. Most accomplishments are only noteworthy in comparison to others. We are always comparing ourselves with others. In chapter 2 we discussed how destructive it is comparing our kids with others. Unfortunately, the world is already doing it and at such a fast speed that we fail to notice it. Do we not care about having more Instagram followers and likes on our posts as compared to our buddies? Don't we remember that famous dialogue from the movie '3 Idiots' that tells us that we feel sad when we see our friends doing better than us in exams? Naturally, it hurts to think that way and that is the reason why we keep telling our children that it is not the case. We hear, "Just do your best." "Your competition is solely with yourself." The beauty of such statements is that they are meant to discourage you from trying in the first place but not from avoiding competition. Thankfully, our world is not one in which survival requires the murder of others. The benefit of our societies is that even in the absence of direct competition, there are plenty of possibilities and resources for every one of us to survive.

However, never give in to the widespread misconception that there is no competition. Dressing up well attracts other people. We go on interviews to get employment. We only lose and feel down if we don't give our best try and think that there is no competition. Everything that is in demand is priced competitively. And only those who are prepared to put up a real struggle for it may attain the finest.

Life is not fair because we run behind numbers and actions.

A person's ability to influence others is how society evaluates them. When you do anything for a lot of people, you are already valuable. But do we think about ourselves in this manner? No, that is not how we evaluate ourselves. By our thinking, we evaluate ourselves. "I am a good human being", " I am an honest person", I try my best to do good work ", though these feelings and thoughts may help us to be at peace with ourselves and we can sleep at night without taking much worry. The hard truth is that the outside world does not see us this way. And just reflect do we judge others also based on what they feel about themselves? Not really! When it comes to others, we also look for their actions. Having good intentions is irrelevant. Let's accept that when it comes to the real world our internal feelings of responsibility, love, and honor are worthless. What precisely have you accomplished for the world through these feelings? Any respect that society bestows upon us originates from other people's self-serving viewpoints. Society rewards a cunning marketing agent more than an honest sweeper who keeps our surroundings clean for us. A model receives higher compensation than a nurse. Why? As a result of the greater impact and rarity of those abilities. We like to believe that people who perform the best work are rewarded by society. However, social reward is only a result of networking, numbers, and the market. The number of individuals you influence ultimately determines your reward. If your book is unpublished, you are nothing. The moment you write a book that is a best-seller, the world is interested in you because you have written a best-seller. Regretfully, this principle holds for all abilities, even shady ones: flatter your friends, you might just make them happy; flatter to all your colleagues including your team leader you might just become the next team leader. You might find this offensive but that's how the world is running. Your worth is determined by your actions and the number of individuals you can go and influence. That's the reason why everybody wants to be on YouTube nowadays. Should you refuse to acknowledge this, then the world's assessment will appear incredibly unjust.

Life is not fair, and your idea of fairness is a bit flawed.

Our society is deep into the concept of right and wrong, good and bad. That's why our parents and teachers are always telling us to do good things. Be a good boy or good girl. We all have a very high sense of right and wrong. That's why we always want referees/ judges/umpires to decide for us that we are right. But the reality is quite different. Many students study hard but don't get good scores. Many people work hard but don't get success in their lives. Many people love a person deeply but do not get the same love from the other person. The problem is not that life is not fair to you, but your idea of fairness is a bit flawed. Just think about the person whom you loved a lot but did not respond in the same way the way you loved her or him. What is the possible reason? You think you have honest love, and you are ready to do anything for her or him. But why do you think that you are the only person feeling this way? There can be many people in that person's life who say or feel the same way. There can be many people who are better than you in terms of knowledge, skills, looks, etc. Now think about what your chances are of getting loved. For what reason do you think the person will select you just because you feel you have true feelings? You may find that important, but it is not your decision; it is theirs. We often tell others that this person, say your boss or your neighbour or your teacher is not good with you. They are not fair to you because they don't like you. Their conclusions are unjust. And biased since they do not concur with you! Just ask yourself one straight question: Are you the world's foremost authority on everything? Are you always, right? Yes, I agree that there are biased, bad people around us who trouble us because of their unfair behaviour but not all people you don't like are bad. Most people, in situations that differ from you, are only attempting to do the best they can. Perhaps they have knowledge that you do not, their perception is different than yours and maybe they are better than you. Still, you would say that this person is not fair to me. Life is not fair to me. Why? Just because your idea of fairness is a bit flawed!

How to react when Life is not fair?

Only Parents and Teachers can set an example for this mindset. So, stop becoming upset when someone else experiences happiness even when you experience setbacks. Life is not a limited pie that shrinks as each person receives a smaller portion of the larger, happier pie. Rather, we need to cultivate a mindset in our households and schools that says there is enough joy for everyone. Kids that grow up in this kind of environment are less territorial and possessive of their belongings. We begin by teaching children to share when they are young. Children will grow very insecure if they are told to hide their items for themselves rather than share them with others. Additionally, I can tell you that they will grow up as a biased person and will not be able to treat others equally. They would not view life that way, even if it were entirely fair. Sharing may be as easy for some as pulling teeth for others, but when goods and privileges are viewed as gifts rather than rights, life is much more enjoyable.

Let the children experience that life is unfair too: To maintain harmony, many parents and teachers exhaust themselves attempting to keep things fair amongst their kids. You, the parents and teachers, are the losers in that conflict. Giving your children a taste of reality at a young age and emphasizing that life is unfair and that it is not your responsibility to make it fair for them are the best things you can do for them. They experience nice things occasionally, and their siblings experience bad things occasionally. "Rejoice with one another" is the secret to appreciating both moments.

This is only possible if you set an example of gracious living for your children and make it the norm in your household and classrooms. By taking this action, you remove one of the main causes of sibling and peer rivalry from the deck. When children realize that life is not fair and, more crucially, that it is not even meant to be fair, they will fight far less.

Don't Be A Parent, Don't Be A Friend: Be A Life Coach

- There are certain things in life that we can never change, and they will always be unjust.

- What children really "need" is love and the unwavering reassurance that, despite the injustices of life, they are loved and have a place in the world. We all need a safe place for our children to fall.

- One of the hardest lessons we can teach our kids is that life will not be always "fair." Nevertheless, there is power in letting go of the things we cannot control.

- Perhaps the most significant lesson of all is that although life is not fair, it is nevertheless beautiful.

* * *

CHAPTER 6

Childhood Is In Crisis

The rain had stopped for a day. Safran, an 11-year-old boy from a government high school in Punjab was on his way to school. He was walking carefully as roads were filled up with water as there had been consistent rain for the last two days. As he started crossing a bridge which was quite narrow, he saw a biker coming, realizing that his dress may spoiled due to a speeding bike he ran at his best. Despite his best efforts, he got drenched by to speeding bike. If the biker had slowed down, he would have saved his dress from getting ruined. He lost his cool and shouted at the biker. The biker, Ravi, a 16-year-old boy from his school had zoomed past him and then returned to him. A small argument turned into a dispute. Ravi threatened him that he would beat him after school hours. After school hours Safaan rushed to his uncle Bittu who had a criminal history. Bittu had gone out of the town. Safaan picked up a knife from Bittu's shop and started walking towards his home, thinking that he would teach Ravi a lesson. But before he could reach home, he saw Ravi coming on his bike with his friend. Ravi stopped his bike in front of Safaan. Before Ravi could get out of the bike Safaan attacked him and stabbed him to death. His friend Anil ran away looking at the rage in the eyes of Safaan. The next day most of the media houses ran this news with a headline: An 11-year-old boy killed 16-year-old boy. People read the news and there was discussion that kids have lost values, and our society needs moral values.

Maybe they are true but as an educator who has worked with thousands of kids in the last ten years, I can confidently say this has less to do with moral values. Our children desperately need lessons in handling their emotions. As an Educator I worked with thousands of teachers across the country to work on Foundational literacy and numeracy in elementary grades. No doubt the overall quality of education has gone down in the last few decades and the government has realised it hence there are mass-scale projects to address this issue. Unfortunately, there is a more alarming crisis in our education: Emotional Crisis. And sadly, there is no curriculum to handle this issue. We are taking the lives of our children for granted.

Parents and Teachers accept that children are very different nowadays. They often talk about social media addiction and video games and then they also share about the resistance they get from children on the issues of rules and values. They also talk about different kinds of patterns and behaviours they notice in new generations like spending less time in playgrounds or talking to them. What Parents and Teachers do not highlight are the mental health issues that are growing at a very high rate among children.

When we listen to some of the stories Parents and Teachers talk about their children, it becomes clear that the picture is quite dark. Almost every second child is going through some emotional issues. The gravity may vary but most children are in some form of mental health issues. And sometimes we adults acknowledge that this happening, but we just blame it on social media. We know we are just helpless and trapped.

During my tenure as school principal of a highly democratic school, I started a class for teenagers named Adolescence class. It was one of the most awaited classes for the kids every week. The design of the class was that kids would write their questions, worries, and doubts on any topic related to their lives. No academic issues, nothing related to subjects. Anything that has a linkage to their lives. And the kind of questions kids used to ask were just shocking. This class was for grade 6 to grade 10 children. Most of their questions were about the use of drugs, sex, anxiety, stress, and depression. Within these large topics there used to be questions about fear, sadness, hopelessness, anger management, and violence. All these topics are somehow related to mental health issues. And this is the story of every school and every home. There are clear signs that there is a drastic increase in emotional and mental health issues among children. Surprisingly most teachers and well-known educators often dismiss these issues stating that even for minor things kids nowadays get worried and label it as a mental health issue and hence we should not get overwhelmed with such cases where kids share mild symptoms of worry and stress.

Has childhood changed?

Let's talk about one of the major reasons for mental health issues among teenagers as cited by parents and teachers -the influence of social media. No doubt social media has changed our lives.

In the 90s it was Television that was at the centre of our lives. Everyone remembers watching Ramayan, Mahabharata, Chandarkanta, Shanti, and Swabhiman on Television. We used to go to other people's homes to watch cricket matches. TV was no doubt an indispensable part of our life.

In early 2000, mobiles entered our lives in India. Basic phones without any access to the Internet. We used to talk endlessly on the phone with our close ones. Slowly, computers started entering our lives also.

After the arrival of smartphones, around 2010 life changed dramatically. It was this time when the concept of the virtual world entered our lives. Children started preferring the online world as compared to the real world. And the access to smartphones among children has also increased drastically. Around 50% of children in the country have now access to smartphones. Also, the time spent online is increasing. The option of staying online 24 x 7 has just been crazy. I don't remember when the last time I saw a teenager just sitting alone and doing nothing. I don't think you will find any person in any restaurant waiting for his or her order without flipping his phone. Even when kids are studying at home or talking to each other or even while riding vehicles they are paying attention to their smartphones. Are these patterns of children's behaviour not sufficient to tell us that childhood has changed, and we must accept it?

If we accept that childhood has drastically changed in the last decade mostly because of the influence of smartphones we should also look at the dangers that smartphones bring to childhood.

Where are the social connections?

When children enter classes 4 and 5, they start looking at other children of their age group. They need to bond with other children and work in groups. In this process, they pick up many important skills which are important in their lives. One of these highly useful skills is the ability to make social connections. The kind of social life children live online is far more isolated than the life they live in the real world. The quality of relationships they make on social media is negligible and that makes them feel starving for more and more connections in a virtual world. Result: Most of the children who stay on social media always feel alone as compared to the kids who connect with their families and friends in the real world.

Why don't children break their comfort zones?

If you ask any person how he became confident and fearless, the answer is through experience and action. When we try new things, when we explore new ways to learn we learn something interesting. We get the confidence to try more new things. We start reaching out to new people as per our experiences. We understand how beautiful the world is, and we accept diversity as a driving force in the colourful world around us. Unfortunately, due to social media, we are a constant source of bad news, threats, and dangers. Instead of going out, we look for safety which is our natural need. And the priority is to keep the most vulnerable group safe. Hence, we did not encourage our children to go out often. We want them to stay at home. We want them to learn something online in their comfort zones. Result: Children don't break their comfort zones to work hard in the real world. That's why most teachers and parents often say that nowadays children are not ready to put in extra effort.

Generation with attention disorder:

I am sure many of my fellow teachers and parents may disagree on the word disorder here but is it not a disorder when a child is not able to stay away from a smartphone even for five minutes?

I will tell you a funny example to talk more about it. As a child, I used to wait for guests to come home because every time there was a new guest there were sweets at home. So, in the evening when my father would return home, I would just sit in the veranda of my house and wait to see whether he is alone, or someone has joined him to visit our home. Recently I saw my landlord's child sitting in the veranda of his house and asked him whether he was waiting for someone to come. Interestingly he said yes and when I enquired whom, he said, OTP. He wanted to buy something online, but OTP was not coming due to a poor network. Isn't it funny and true that we wait for endless notifications on our phones? Let us try to mark some of the most common notifications that we keep getting on our smartphones all the time.

- WhatsApp messages
- Instagram
- Facebook
- Telegram
- Twitter
- YouTube
- Tinder
- Emails
- Newsflash.

We are always on high alert because of these constant alerts. Ironically this alert does not increase our attention span but rather reduces our attention span which I am referring to as Attention disorder.

The world of addiction: What's more?

Due to extremely high screen time, the children often want to remain in a state of high dopamine that they get either through online addiction or through drugs. Yes, along with online addiction, another major danger to our children is easy access to drugs. Every school, and college in any part of the country has people who supply drugs to young children. These two kinds of addiction: Addiction to the online world and drug addiction are destroying our children's lives. We must admit that the childhood is in crisis.

Don't Be A Parent, Don't Be A Friend: Be A Counsellor

If we all agree that our children are in danger, we must take a pledge to help our children come out of mental health issues that are linked to drug and online addiction.

Connect with nature:

The most powerful force in this world is nature. Can we not connect our children more with nature? Nature has immense power to heal anything. Many of us know that and have experienced that. Can't we do something to bring children closer to nature? Should we not start doing nature walks for the children? What about treks and hikes to nearby mountains? And the rule will be simple: No Smartphones, No Drugs, and get addicted to Nature around us.

Collective actions:

Another powerful force in the world that derives us in our lives is the power of community. Schools and families are the most beautiful communities. Can we take collective action towards these addictions? All those who are part of spiritual communities show remarkable changes in their lives in terms of finding peace. How? It is the power of being together that pushes people to come out of their struggles. Should schools not start events where kids spend time on face-to-face things rather than being alone on smartphones?

* * *

CHAPTER 7

Be A Friend And Be A Parent Too

In the last 6 chapters, I kept telling you not to be a parent and not to be a friend. But is it possible not to be a parent and a friend to our children? These two are the loveliest of all the relationships we have in our life. As much as I say that don't be a parent, it will not change the truth that you will remain a parent to your child. How much I say that don't be a friend, you will continue to remain the lifelong friend of your child. The point I wanted to make was that being a parent and being a friend is difficult because there is such a huge responsibility on your shoulders. Most of the people who struggle emotionally in life somehow raise their fingers on their childhood.

The influence our parents had on us is profound and hence it should be mandatory for all parents to build their understanding of parenting. Unfortunately, there is no school and there is no class that teaches us about parenting. For teachers, there are training programs, but the focus is mostly on subject and pedagogical content knowledge.

The general pedagogy and understanding of childhood are often put at last. In many cases, parents are not even aware of some basic rules of parenting. They find it so difficult to handle kids and the easiest way for them is to just punish their kids. They don't realize that punishment would damage their kids for life long. As said in previous chapters also that the intention of many parents and teachers is not to harm their children because parents and teachers are the only two kinds of people in this world who always want their kids to succeed. But the impact of such acts of beating is so harmful that the whole life of many kids gets spoiled. Therefore, to be a good parent we must detach ourselves from the existing stereotypical role of being a parent. Rather we must play different kinds of roles to be a good parent and a lifelong friend to our children. Let's revise the roles we discuss in the last 6 chapters.

- **Be A Mentor**: In chapter one, we discussed how fear is one of the most horrible things that can destroy our lives and instead of putting our children into this dark zone we must help them to get out of this disease.

- **Be A Spiritual Guru**: In chapter two, we discussed our comparisons lead to suffering and our children develop low self-esteem. Hence it is important to be in the role of spiritual guru to guide our kids to embrace the beautiful life and succeed in whatever pursuit we take up.

- **Be A Facilitator**: In chapter three, we found out that one of the central points of all parenting is how we talk to our children. The power of words cannot be ignored in parenting and hence it is crucial to get into the shoes of a facilitator who can help the child to be empathetic, confident, and happy in life.

- **Be A Trainer**: Chapter four tells us that mistakes are bound to happen in life. Instead of pointing out mistakes, we should help our kids to accept mistakes and learn from them. We must help our kids in this the way trainers train great athletes.

- **Be A Life Coach**: Chapter five reminds us that life is full of ups and downs. There can be moments when our children are not at the best of their lives. Life can be unfair to them sometimes. How can we instil lifelong lessons in them? We must play the role of a life coach here.

- **Be A Counsellor**: In chapter six, we realized that the present generation is under high stress and anxiety. If we look at online addiction that often leads to substance use, we need to think about childhood under crisis. Parents must work like counsellors to help their kids come out of the dark world.

Now you must be wondering how difficult it is to be a real parent. Don't forget we are not just parents but at the same time, we are fulfilling different responsibilities in the family, workplace, society, etc. That makes us so much busy with so many things that it becomes difficult for us to pay attention to small aspects of parenting and because of this we fail to acknowledge the joy of being a parent and a friend to our children.

In this chapter, we will talk about the situations when we just must be a parent and friend.

Be A Friend:

We human beings feel best when are physically and emotionally safe and free. Think of the situations when we are with our friends. What do we do? We party and cook things together for dinner, we learn to try new dishes. We dance together. We gossip without fear of being judged. When we play games together with our friends, we improve our skills and enjoy ourselves so much that we don't want to go back home. Sometimes we create new things together and we feel so excited to try new things. As friends, we give freedom to each other to express our thoughts freely and that's why we want to be with our friends all the time. Our friends accept us the way we are. We feel deeply connected with our friends and share deeper feelings with them. They don't judge us and don't compare us with others. We are special to them.

There are endless moments in our lives when we can be like friends to our children and help them grow into remarkable human beings. Here are some of the key opportunities for this role.

Play like friends:

Can there be a child who does not like to play? There can be some cases where a child has a serious setback in life and he or she does not want to play. Otherwise, most of the kids just love to play. Play is key to remaining happy in life. What are the reasons why kids love to play so much?

One of the most exciting things when kids are very young is that they create their own rules while playing. They try so many new things spontaneously. There is no one around them to tell this right and this is wrong. Even when the peers argue they handle things. Sometimes there are fights too but they forget soon and start playing again.

The ability to adapt, adjust, and handle different social interactions with others grows so well during these free plays.

In the previous chapter, we discussed in detail the dangers of the online world. We must bring our children back to playgrounds and play with them like kids.

In the NCERT English textbook for grade 10, there is a chapter when a dog is sick because it never indulges in any kind of play. Its owner loves the dog so much that it is pampered and hence only fed all the time. Our kids are like pets, these dogs who are fed by social media all the time. In this story a veterinary doctor makes the dog play all the time and very soon the dog becomes healthier. We parents should get our kids to run, dance, jump, and enjoy the play. This is possible when we behave like their friends and will not judge them for their stupidity.

The bonds between friends during play are deep. They fight, argue, abuse, and compete but at the end of the game, they are buddies. Play the game and play it well. The social bond we develop during play teaches us to be with people.

We want our kids to be thoughtful. Right? While engaging in different games of play our children develop to think out of the box also. They get so immersed in the game that they start thinking beyond normal. I often play cards with kids, and I lose all the time because kids around me come up with such a creative strategy that I fail to crack them. Many of the kids while playing realize their real passion. They start to know themselves more. The things they like, dislike, and their interests all come in front of them. I remember my nephew who is in grade 5 saying 'I wish I just stay with fish all the time'. He plays with fish for hours and he knows so much about them that even a Master degree student of Zoology cannot tell.

If we want our kids to be creative, we must focus on the power of imagination. Imagination has no end. When kids are involved in any kind of play, they are in a state of imagination. In early grades when kids are encouraged to play with colours they come up with such a creative idea.

I remember a grade 2 kid making red colour mangoes in her notebook. When I asked how a mango can be red. She replied that she is eating the mangoes with chutney which her mother gives to customers when they eat momos. I was amazed to hear this.

If we parents play like friends for three hours a week with our children, I can guarantee that many of our children's miseries in life will be resolved because we will be able to know them better. We will understand their needs, and their personalities to the deepest and they will never shy away from sharing anything with us.

Watch cinema together:

A few years ago, I was watching the movie 'The Boy with the striped pajamas'. It is one of my favourite movies and I have seen it more than hundreds of times. Some of the scenes just keep coming in front of my eyes all the time. As I started watching this movie a girl of 13 years old came to meet me. I told her to watch the movie despite knowing that she would not like it because it's a serious genre movie and does not match her taste. Somehow, she sat there. The movie was over. Tears were down my cheek. This girl did not say a word and returned to her home. I knew that she would not like the movie.

For the next few days, I could not meet the girl as I was out of the station. After a few weeks, this girl came to meet me again and asked me about the title of the movie. I asked whether she liked the movie. She said that not only did she like the movie, but she had been thinking about the movie all the time. She feels how difficult life can be for some children. She also told me that she wants to watch some more of such movies. This girl proved me wrong. Cinema has the power to change the way we think.

We enjoy movies with friends. Can we parents be not like friends who take our children to watch cinema and not just garden variety cinema but some meaningful cinema that can help our children to develop new perspectives towards life?

Be A Parent: Only Parents and Teachers Can Do this

In the last few chapters, I have been bombarding you with all the points of not behaving like a parent and the purpose is to help your children do well in their lives. That's what parents want for their children to do well in their lives.

Other than this there is another important aspect of parenting that some parents may ignore but largely parents want their kids to become, which is good human beings.

Yes, we all want a good society. Are we all not disturbed by what is happening in the world around us? Girls being raped brutally, murders, robbery, hate crimes, injustice, even war among nations- do we want to stay in this kind of society?

We may say that yes, these things are happening but what can we do about them? We are not part of these problems.

Well, it would be unwise to think that we are not part of the problems and that we cannot do anything about these issues. I think parents and teachers are the most powerful people in this world because they are the ones who build individuals, societies, and nations.

A few years ago, during covid times I remember a highly insightful conversation between a grade 1 student and his teacher. Online classes were going on, and the topic was 'colours'. The teacher asked the kids to share their favourite colours. All the kids were sharing their favourite colours. The moment a girl started sharing that she likes black colour and she has a lot of black colour sketch pens, her classmate jumped in the middle of a conversation and said that he hates black colour. The teacher asked him to speak more. The kid responded by saying that he does not like people who are dark because they are not good-looking. They are bad. He does not like to be friends with kids who are dark. He even said that his mother gives him cream every day so that he becomes fairer. It was so funny that the kid told everything with full zest that his mother had taught him. The teacher asked another question to him- I am also dark, so you also don't like me, right? Now the kid got stuck and just said 'No ma'am I like you, you are good.

As Parents, we start the foundation of citizenship in our kids. What kind of citizen our kids will become depends entirely on our dialogue with them especially on the topic of diversity.

Right from an early age kids start noticing some differences in their surroundings. How their peers are different. Some differences based on sex, colour, and body are easily visible. As they grow old, they start knowing about all kinds of differences that are deep in our societies. Differences based on caste, religion, region, etc are all familiar to children as they often listen about them in their surroundings.

Here we commit a serious mistake as teachers and parents by thinking that children are not interested in these topics, and these are not for them. We think that we should avoid bringing up the topics of differences with them as they are young and will not be interested or would not be able to handle them. Whenever kids bring up such topics, we just shut them down. We fail to understand that differences are right there in front of kids and the more we ignore them, the more kids will think about them. Unfortunately, as parents and teachers, we avoid talking about them, but kids pick our behaviour on these topics from us only. In many families males dominate females and kids practice the same. In many schools, one kind of religious festival is promoted, and children start believing that our religion is superior. In many communities, groups are based on caste and kids start believing in caste discrimination. Just imagine kids and communities growing up with so much discrimination around them and not getting the right answers. They will practice what our society is practicing. And then we expect them to become better human beings?

How should we teach our children to be good citizens?

If we want our kids to become good citizens, we must teach them the following things:

Knowledge is not just information:

In this age of social media, it is so difficult to get the right facts. We just believe what is being told to us on the internet and most of the time we just believe in it. As a parent and teachers, we must provide the right facts to our kids. If we don't do this, we will grow them with wrong facts which will cause them to develop wrong beliefs about others. For example, most of us say that Hindi is our national language which is a wrong fact. Hindi is our official language, not our national language. There is no national language in our country. Our country is full of diversity and the eight schedule of our constitution mention that there is a total of 22 official languages in our country.

Now think how this fact is linked to becoming a better human being. This small fact brings the idea that our country is a diversity. Our constitution is telling us that we must appreciate diversity. If we force anything on anyone it is a real danger to our diversity. The whole concept of unity in diversity gets challenged here if we are asking anyone to forcefully do something.

There are so many things about the world around us that are presented in the form of wrong facts to us and our kids. It is the most important duty of a parent to provide the right facts to his or her kid.

Once our children have the right facts, does it mean they will understand things easily.

They will be able to understand things well once they see things from different perspectives and that will broaden their understanding. The more they will be able to comprehend, the more they will be able to apply this understanding in their day-to-day life.

As their information, understanding, and application of things improve, they must analysis well. They should not accept things as it is rather should do detailed analyses of each aspect of a thing. This will finally help them to make better decisions in life.

Most of the cases of unjust in life happen when we fail to decide things thoughtfully. We just succumb to what people around us are doing. Without giving any second thoughts we just believe what is being told to us. And that is one of the primary reasons for discrimination-a blind faith in beliefs that we are superior, and others are not.

Speaking about social values:

One of the most complicated topics that we all human beings struggle with on a day-to-day basis. Can we parents simplify this a bit for our kids so that they don't grow into confused human beings who are then brainwashed by others? Can we stick to some core principles of human kindness, love, brotherhood, openness, and cooperation?

We must make our kids curious about these things. For example, if there is a child who is dark in colour and everyone calls him by his name based on his colour, what should we do as parents? Should we give our kids a long lecture on good and bad? Should we warn our kids that calling someone dark can be problematic?

As a parent and teachers, we must talk about social values. We must help the children understand how a society is built and why everyone needs to be treated equally in this society. We human beings cannot live in isolation and are interdependent and hence any step towards discrimination will set an example for others to practice and that's how a culture is built. The kind of culture we build makes our social values.

How do help our children practice good values?

Though the first two steps a) making us aware of things around us by getting the right information and b) understanding the importance of values in our lives are fundamental in helping our kids become better citizens, the last step starts bringing real change in our children's behaviour. It is about how we live our lives. What we practice in our lives is what matters the most. Sometimes we get to meet many learned people who understand things well and set high values but struggle to do real action in life. That's why practice is so crucial to see the change.

We can use these steps to help our children become better human beings.

Observe:

Observation is not just noticing things but thinking about what you notice. And it does not come naturally. The first two steps of getting aware of things and understanding values help in this a lot. We must ask kids to start observing things minutely. What did you observe in the field? Did you notice anything in the bus? Did you see anything different there? Could you sense stereotypical behaviour in that place?

Asking children to observe how the world runs around them is so crucial in making them a better human being.

Questioning:

Help the kids to ask different kinds of questions whenever they notice any form of difference in their surroundings. Why do you think they don't eat food in Rinki's house? Why does she always wear a salwar -kameez? Why there are so less men in this shop? The more kids start asking questions, the more they will look for possible answers. They will not accept things blindly. They will not become followers of others but rather look for their answers to a variety of questions.

Empathize:

Finally, ask your children to reflect on themselves. How would you feel if someone said that your height is not good? How would you answer to someone who tells you that you are from another state and should not stay here? Would you stand for a girl if boys were teasing her in the street? How would you feel if your sister were in her place?

As parents, if we practice these three things of observation, questioning, and empathizing things to any social problem around us our kids will become extremely aware, sensitive, responsible, and practical human beings who will surely make our society a better place to live.

This is something that only parents and teachers can do. That's why they are the real builders of the nation.

* * *